Puppies come in all shapes and sizes. They are easy to spot almost anywhere you see people—in yards, in the park, or walking down the street.

Puppies make great friends, and though they may look different, they all have one thing in common—they love to play!

◀ Terrier Mix

American Pit Bull Terriers

A puppy's
brothers and
sisters are
its first
playmates.

Bull Dogs

PUPPIES

Boston Terrier

Sarah Hines Stephens

Maltese

Puppies can be all one color or several colors. They might be white, black, brown, or gold.

Bernese Mountain Dog

There are so many different kinds of puppies, it is hard to pick a favorite.

Lhasapoo

Pembroke Welsh Corgi

Whether outside in snow or
grass, puppies love fresh air.

Terrier Mix

In fact, puppies love to play
anywhere—and with anything!

Golden Retrievers

Puppies
have very
sensitive
noses—great
for sniffing
out fun.

Maltapoo

Jack Russell Terrier

Puppies also hear very well.
Did somebody say "playtime"?

◀ *Chihuahua*

Australian Shepherd

Puppies like to get into things.

Puggle

Puppies love to chew on toys and also on shoes, so watch out!

Golden Retriever

Cocker Spaniel

Puppies pant to cool off.
Time for a water break!

German Shepherd

How about a snack, too?
Mmmm, delicious!

After a busy day playing, puppies like to hang out.

Shepherd Mix

Chesapeake Bay Retriever

Jack Russell Terrier

Puppies are growing fast and need lots of rest. They can sleep up to 20 hours a day!

Cocker Spaniel

Shepherd Mix

But when puppies wake up,
they're ready to play again!

Chocolate Labrador Retrievers

Let's play together!

Silver Tabby Piebalds and Brown Tabby

Let's explore together!

After a nice
rest, it is time
to go explore
some more!

Tortoiseshell Longhair

Silver Tabby

Black Golden Tabby Blotched

There is nothing better than a cozy cat nap.

Bicolor Tabby

Lots of play
can make
kittens sleepy.

Mackerel Tabby

Tortoiseshell Shorthair

Mackerel Tabby

Bicolor British Shorthair

After a busy day, kittens like to relax.

Peek-a-boo,
kittens.
We see you!

Calico

Bicolor British Shorthair

Cream Siamese

Kittens enjoy a game
of hide and seek.

Red Tabby

They're always looking
for a fun adventure.

Black Shorthair

Kittens love to
get into things, like
baskets and hats.

Can you
keep a secret?
If you have
something to
say, kittens
are all ears.

British Longhair

Red Tabby Piebald

Brown Tabby

And talk about nosy! Kittens can always sniff out fun.

Tortoiseshell and White

Blue Tabby

Kittens see very well. They look all around to make sure they don't miss anything.

Mackerel Tabby

Mackerel Tabby

Tall grass, piano keys—there are
so many fun things to explore!

Chocolate Bicolor

Kittens
also love to
explore on
their own.

Tortoiseshell Shorthair

Siamese

Kittens share
their first
adventures
with their
brothers
and sisters.

Mackerel Tabbies

Have you ever had a kitten
curl up in your lap for a
nap, felt the rough tongue of
a tiny cat when it kissed you,
or heard the happy rumble
of a kitten's purr? Kittens are
warm balls of joy that love to
cuddle and romp.

Curious kittens also love
to explore. You may find
them playing hide and seek,
climbing high on a branch,
or snuggling up under your
blankets—resting up for their
next fun adventure.

KITTENS

Bicolor Mackerel Shorthair

Sarah Hines Stephens

SCHOLASTIC